Acknowledgements

First and foremost, I offer my deepest gratitude to God, whose boundless grace, wisdom, and love have made the creation of this book possible. His unwavering presence has been my constant source of strength, inspiration, and encouragement throughout this journey. I am forever thankful for His guidance and blessings every step of the way.

To my mom, Apostle Genise Rodgers, thank you for your unshakable faith in me and your relentless encouragement. Your wisdom, prayers, and love have been a guiding light in my life, and I am deeply grateful for the foundation you've given me. Your belief in my dreams has inspired me to persevere and walk confidently in my purpose.

To my Mary Kay Director, Dawn, and my Mary Kay Team Leader, Debbie, your mentorship and support have been invaluable. Dawn, your leadership and ability to empower others have left an indelible mark on my journey. Debbie, your unwavering positivity and dedication to our team have been a source of motivation and joy. Both of you have shown me what it means to lead with grace, passion, and authenticity, and I am honored to have learned from you.

To my family and friends, thank you for being my greatest cheerleaders. Your unwavering love and belief in me have been my anchor during this endeavor, reminding me that I am never alone in my pursuits. Your encouragement has fueled my passion and kept me grounded through the ups and downs of this journey.

A heartfelt thank you to my editor and publishing team for their expertise, dedication, and attention to detail. Your hard work has brought this book to life, and I am truly grateful for your support and partnership.

To my readers, thank you for embarking on this journey with me. It is my hope that the words within these pages inspire, uplift, and encourage you to embrace your unique path with confidence and determination.

Hey Girl! You can sell

A 10-Chapter Guide to Becoming a Confident, Successful Saleswoman

Dr. Monique Rodgers

Hey Girl! You can sell

Dr. Monique Rodgers

United States of America

Published by Shooting Stars Publishing House 2024
Copyright © 2024 Dr. Monique Rodgers
All Rights Reserved.

ISBN:

This book has been published with all reasonable efforts taken to make the material error-free after the consent of the author. No part of this book shall be used, reproduced in any manner whatsoever without written permission from the author, except in the case of brief quotations embodied in critical articles and reviews.

The Author of this book is solely responsible and liable for its content including but not limited to the views, representations, descriptions, statements, information, opinions, and references. The Content of this book shall not constitute or be construed or deemed to reflect the opinion or expression of the Publisher or Editor. Neither the Publisher nor Editor endorse or approve the Content of this book or guarantee the reliability, accuracy or completeness of the Content published herein and do not make any representations or warranties of any kind, express or implied, including but not limited to the implied warranties of merchantability, fitness for a particular purpose. The Publisher and Editor shall not be liable whatsoever for any errors, omissions, whether such errors or omissions result from negligence, accident, or any other cause or claims for loss or damages of any kind, including without limitation, indirect or consequential loss or damage arising out of use, inability to use, or about the reliability, accuracy or sufficiency of the information contained in this book

Lastly, I dedicate this book to those who dream big, persevere through challenges, and believe in the power of transformation. May this story remind you of the strength that lies within you and the beauty of embracing your journey.

With deepest gratitude,

Dr. Monique Rodgers

Contents

Acknowledgements……………………………………..Page 3

Introduction…………………………………………….Page 7

Chapter One……………………………………………Page 11

Chapter Two……………………………………………Page 18

Chapter Three………………………………………….Page 27

Chapter Four…………………………………………...Page 37

Chapter Five……………………………………………Page 48

Chapter Six…………………………………………….Page 59

Chapter Seven………………………………………….Page 72

Chapter Eight…………………………………………...Page 85

Chapter Nine…………………………………………...Page 100

Chapter Ten……………………………………………Page 113

Finale…………………………………………………..Page 126

About the Author……………………………………...Page 140

Introduction

Unleash Your Inner Power

Welcome to "**Hey Girl, You Can Sell**"—a transformative guide that's about to change the way you think about sales, success, and, most importantly, yourself.

This is not just another book about sales tactics and techniques. It's a rallying cry for women who are ready to step into their power, claim their confidence, and dominate in an industry where our voices deserve to be heard. Whether you're new to the world of sales or a seasoned professional looking to elevate your game, this book will give you the tools, strategies, and mindset shifts needed to break through barriers and achieve unparalleled success.

Why? Because selling isn't just a skill—it's an art. And you, my friend, are a masterpiece in the making.

Let's get one thing straight: sales isn't about fitting into a mold or pretending to be someone you're not. It's about embracing who you are—your authenticity, your passion, your unique strengths—and using them to connect with others in a way that feels natural and powerful.

In this book, we're not just going to talk about how to sell; we're going to talk about how to win. You'll learn how to overcome self-doubt, turn challenges into opportunities, and confidently approach every interaction with the belief that you have exactly what it takes to succeed.

You'll discover how to:

- Shift your mindset from hesitant to unstoppable.
- Build genuine relationships that lead to long-term success.
- Handle rejection with resilience and grace.
- Tap into your natural strengths and become a magnetic force in your industry.

But this journey isn't just about numbers, quotas, or commissions. It's about discovering what's possible when you believe in yourself and your ability to create change—not just for yourself, but for the people you serve.

Because sales is more than a transaction. It's an opportunity to make an impact, solve problems, and transform lives.

So, get ready to step into the spotlight, take ownership of your potential, and embrace the truth: you *can* sell—and you can do it with confidence, authenticity, and style.

The world is waiting for what only you can offer. Let's show them what you've got.

Hey girl, let's get started.

Chapter 1
The Mindset Shift – Embrace Your Inner Saleswoman

Selling isn't about slick presentations, memorized scripts, or high-pressure tactics. It's about connecting with people, understanding their needs, and helping them find solutions. Whether you're selling a product, a service, or even an idea, success begins with one essential component: your mindset.

The Power of Thinking Like a Saleswoman

To succeed in sales, you must first believe in yourself as a saleswoman. That doesn't mean adopting a "salesy" persona that feels fake or forced. It means stepping into a role where you recognize the value of what you're offering and the potential impact it can have on others. When you understand this, you're no longer just "selling"—you're serving.

Sales is not a battlefield where you try to outsmart your customers. Instead, it's a partnership. Imagine yourself as a trusted guide, helping others navigate their challenges and find the best solution. When you shift your mindset to focus on service rather than selling, everything changes.

Sales Is About Solutions, Not Pressure

Forget the old stereotype of the pushy salesperson. That approach not only turns people off but also misses the true purpose of sales. When you push a product without considering the customer's needs, you're not building trust—you're burning bridges.

Instead, approach every interaction with curiosity and empathy. Ask yourself:

- What does this person truly need?

- How can my product or service make their life better?

When you start thinking this way, you become more than a salesperson. You become a problem-solver, and people love problem-solvers.

Turning "No" Into a Stepping Stone

Let's be honest—hearing "no" is part of the game. But here's the secret: every "no" is a step closer to a "yes." The key is how you respond to rejection.

A "no" doesn't mean you've failed; it simply means the timing or offer wasn't right for that person. It's not personal—it's situational. Instead of seeing rejection as the end of the road, see it as valuable feedback.

- Was the offer clear enough?
- Did you understand the customer's needs well?

- Could you refine your approach for the next opportunity?

Each "no" teaches you something, and every lesson brings you closer to success.

Confidence Is Your Superpower

Confidence is non-negotiable in sales. People buy from those they trust, and trust starts with believing in yourself and what you're offering. If you don't believe in your product, why should anyone else?

Confidence doesn't mean you have to be perfect or have all the answers. It means you approach each situation with assurance in your abilities and a genuine belief in the value you bring. Even if you're new to sales, confidence can come from preparation and passion.

Here are a few ways to build confidence:

1. Know Your Product Inside Out: When you deeply understand your offering, you'll naturally exude confidence.
2. Practice, Practice, Practice: Rehearse your pitches, anticipate objections, and refine your delivery. Practice makes you polished.
3. Celebrate Small Wins: Every step forward, no matter how small, deserves recognition. Small victories build big confidence.

The Positive Thinking Advantage

Your mindset is your greatest asset—or your biggest roadblock. If you approach sales with fear or doubt, it will show in your interactions. On the flip side, a positive mindset can make even challenging situations feel manageable.

Start each day with affirmations that remind you of your value:

- "I have solutions people need."
- "Every conversation is an opportunity."
- "I'm getting better with every experience."

Visualize your success. Imagine yourself closing deals, helping customers, and thriving in your role. This mental rehearsal trains your brain to focus on opportunities instead of obstacles.

Your Journey Starts Here

Embracing your inner saleswoman isn't a one-time decision; it's a daily practice. You're laying the foundation for a journey that will not only transform your career but also build your confidence, resilience, and relationships.

By shifting your mindset to focus on service, embracing rejection as part of the process, and leaning into confidence and positivity, you'll unlock a powerful truth: you have what it takes to succeed in sales.

So, take a deep breath, remind yourself of your worth, and step boldly into your role as a saleswoman. You're not just selling—you're making a difference.

And this is just the beginning.

Chapter 2:

Know Your Product – Confidence Comes from Knowledge

Sales success doesn't happen by accident. It's built on a foundation of preparation, expertise, and a deep understanding of what you're offering. If you want to excel in sales, you must become an expert on your product or service. When you know your product inside and out, you'll speak with confidence, handle objections effortlessly, and inspire trust in your customers.

Let's break it down: knowledge isn't just power—it's your superpower in sales.

The Anatomy of Your Product: Features and Benefits

When someone asks, "What's so great about your product?" you need to have a clear, compelling answer. That starts with understanding the two key aspects of any product: **features** and **benefits.**

- **Features** are the facts. They're the specific qualities or characteristics of your product. For example, if you're selling a skincare cream, features might include ingredients like hyaluronic acid or SPF protection.
- **Benefits** answer the all-important question: "What's in it for me?" Benefits explain how those features improve the customer's life. Using the same skincare cream, benefits might include reducing wrinkles or protecting skin from harmful UV rays.

When you're in a sales conversation, focus on the benefits more than the features. Features inform, but benefits sell. People want to know how your product will solve their problem, save them time, or make them feel better.

Understanding the Customer's Perspective

Knowing your product is only half the battle. You also need to understand how it fits into your customer's life. This requires a little empathy and a lot of listening.

Ask yourself:

- Who is my ideal customer?
- What are their pain points?
- How can my product make their life easier, better, or more enjoyable?

When you see your product through the customer's eyes, you'll naturally tailor your pitch to address their needs. You're no longer just selling a product—you're offering a solution.

Mastering the Details

Confidence comes from preparation, and preparation comes from mastering the details. Here's how to level up your product knowledge:

1. **Read the Manual**: This might seem obvious, but many salespeople overlook it. If your product has technical specs, user guides, or training materials, study them. Familiarize yourself with every detail, even the ones that seem trivial. You never know what might resonate with a customer.

2. **Use It Yourself**: Nothing builds authenticity like firsthand experience. If possible, try the product yourself. Your personal insights will make your pitch more relatable and credible.

3. **Understand the Competition**: To position your product effectively, you need to know what else is out there. Research your competitors and understand how your product stands out. Highlight those unique selling points in your conversations.

4. **Ask Questions**: Don't hesitate to reach out to your team, product developers, or customer support for additional insights. The more questions you ask, the better equipped you'll be

to answer your customers' questions.

The Art of Simplifying Complex Information

Not all customers are tech-savvy or familiar with industry jargon. A big part of knowing your product is being able to explain it clearly and simply.

Imagine you're explaining your product to a friend who knows nothing about it. How would you describe it in plain language? This approach ensures that your message is clear, accessible, and impactful.

For example, instead of saying, "Our software uses advanced algorithms to optimize workflow efficiency," try: "Our software helps you get more done in less time by automating repetitive tasks."

Handling Objections with Ease

Even with a deep understanding of your product, you'll face objections. But here's the good news: objections aren't deal-breakers. They're opportunities to showcase your expertise.

When a customer raises a concern, don't panic or get defensive. Instead, use your product knowledge to address their worry confidently and calmly.

For instance, if someone says, "Your product seems expensive," respond with, "I understand it's an investment, and here's why it's worth it..." Then highlight the benefits that justify the cost.

Becoming a Natural Conversationalist

The better you know your product, the more naturally the conversation will flow. You won't have to rely on scripted pitches or canned responses because you'll genuinely understand what you're talking about.

This authenticity makes you more relatable and trustworthy. Customers can sense when you truly believe in what you're selling, and that belief is contagious.

Practice Makes Perfect

Even with thorough preparation, practice is essential. Role-play with colleagues, rehearse your pitch in front of a mirror, or record yourself to identify areas for improvement. The more you practice, the more confident and polished you'll become.

Knowledge + Confidence = Success

When you know your product, you position yourself as a trusted expert. Customers don't just buy products—they buy confidence, solutions, and relationships. By investing the time to master your product, you're setting yourself up for long-term success in sales.

So, dive deep, ask questions, and embrace every opportunity to learn. The more you know, the more confident you'll feel, and that confidence will shine through in every conversation.

Now, let's take what you've learned here and turn it into action. Knowledge isn't just power—it's profit. And you're ready to make it happen.

Chapter 3:

Building Relationships – Sales is About People, Not Just Products

When you strip sales down to its core, it's not about products, quotas, or revenue. It's about people. Behind every transaction is a human being with their own needs, goals, and challenges. The best salespeople know how to connect on a personal level, understanding that relationships are the foundation of long-term success.

In this chapter, we'll explore how to build meaningful relationships, engage in active listening, and genuinely understand your customers. When you master the art of connection, selling becomes a natural extension of the trust and rapport you've established.

The Power of Connection

Think about a time when you bought something from someone you trusted. Maybe it was a friend who recommended a product or a salesperson who took the time to get to know you. How did that experience make you feel? Chances are, it was positive because the interaction was built on connection, not just a sales pitch.

Customers don't want to feel like a number. They want to feel seen, heard, and understood. Building relationships isn't just a strategy—it's the heartbeat of effective sales.

Listening: The Secret Weapon

It might sound cliché, but listening is one of the most powerful tools in your sales arsenal. And we're not talking about passive listening—nodding along while waiting for your turn to talk. We're talking about

active listening, where you're fully present and engaged in the conversation.

Here's how to level up your listening game:

1. **Ask Open-Ended Questions**: Instead of yes-or-no questions, ask ones that encourage customers to share more. For example, "What challenges are you facing right now?" or "What's most important to you in a solution?"

2. **Repeat and Clarify**: Paraphrase what the customer says to show you're listening and ensure you've understood them correctly. For instance, "So, you're looking for something that saves time and is easy to use—did I get that right?"

3. **Read Between the Lines**: Pay attention to tone, body language, and what's not being said. Sometimes, customers reveal as much through their hesitations or emotions as they do through their words.

Understanding Customer Needs

Building relationships requires empathy—the ability to see things from the customer's perspective. Empathy allows you to identify their needs and position your product as the perfect solution.

Here's a simple framework to understand customer needs:

- **Pain Points**: What challenges or problems is the customer trying to solve?

- **Desires**: What outcomes or benefits do they hope to achieve?
- **Priorities**: What matters most to them—cost, convenience, quality, or something else?

By focusing on these three areas, you'll gain a deeper understanding of what drives your customers and how you can meet their needs.

Building Trust Through Authenticity

People can spot a fake from a mile away. If you're overly rehearsed, insincere, or just trying to make a quick sale, customers will feel it—and they'll walk away.

Authenticity is the key to building trust. Here's how to stay real:

1. **Be Honest**: If your product isn't the right fit for someone, say so. Customers will appreciate your integrity and may even come back to you in the future for something else.

2. **Show Vulnerability**: It's okay to admit when you don't have all the answers. If a customer asks a question you're unsure about, respond with, "That's a great question. Let me find out for you."

3. **Share Your Passion**: When you're genuinely excited about what you're selling, it's contagious. Let your enthusiasm shine through in your conversations.

Creating Win-Win Situations

Sales is not a zero-sum game. The goal isn't to "win" at the customer's expense—it's to create value for both parties. When you approach sales as a collaboration rather than a transaction, everyone benefits.

For example:

- If a customer expresses concerns about price, work with them to find a solution that fits their budget without compromising quality.
- If they're unsure about committing, offer a trial period or flexible return policy to build their confidence.

By prioritizing the customer's needs, you'll foster loyalty and strengthen the relationship.

The Follow-Up: Cementing the Connection

Building relationships doesn't end when the deal is closed. In fact, the follow-up is where the magic happens. Staying in touch shows customers that you care about them beyond the transaction.

Here are some simple ways to follow up:

1. **Send a Thank-You Note**: A quick email or handwritten card expressing gratitude can go a long way.

2. **Check In**: Reach out a few weeks after the sale to see how they're doing and if they need any additional support.

3. **Share Value**: Send helpful resources, tips, or updates related to your product. For example, if

you sold them a software subscription, share a guide on maximizing its features.

Building Relationships for the Long Haul

Strong relationships lead to repeat business, referrals, and long-term success. When customers feel valued, they become loyal advocates for you and your product. And loyal advocates aren't just good for business—they're the ultimate testament to the power of connection.

So, remember: sales isn't about closing deals—it's about opening doors. When you prioritize relationships over revenue, the results will speak for themselves.

Putting It Into Practice

Start small. The next time you talk to a customer, focus less on selling and more on connecting. Ask questions, listen intently, and find ways to genuinely add value to their lives.

Because at the end of the day, sales is about people. And when you put people first, success naturally follows.

Let's get out there and make some connections.

Chapter 4:

Mastering Communication – Speak with Purpose

Communication is at the core of every successful interaction, especially in sales. Whether you're presenting a product, addressing concerns, or building rapport, the way you communicate can make or break a deal. Great communication isn't just about what you say—it's how you say it, how you listen, and how you respond.

In this chapter, we'll dive into the art of effective communication, covering verbal and non-verbal techniques, the importance of active listening, and how to guide conversations with purpose and confidence.

The Power of Purposeful Conversations

Every conversation you have in sales should serve a purpose. This doesn't mean being pushy or scripted, but rather approaching discussions with intention. Are you trying to build rapport? Uncover a customer's needs? Demonstrate the value of your product?

When you're clear about your purpose, your communication becomes focused and impactful. Start by asking yourself, **"What do I want this conversation to achieve?"** Then, structure your dialogue to align with that goal.

Verbal Communication: The Words That Close Deals

Speak Clearly and Confidently

Your tone and delivery matter just as much as the words you use. Confidence instills trust. Even if you're nervous, practice speaking with clarity and conviction. Remember, confidence isn't about being loud—it's about being assured in your knowledge and approach.

Simplify Your Message

Avoid jargon or overly complex explanations. Speak in a way that's relatable and easy to understand. The simpler your message, the more likely your customer is to engage with it.

Use Positive Language

The words you choose set the tone of the conversation. Instead of saying, "I'm not sure if this will work," say, "Here's how this solution can address your needs." Positive, affirming language creates a sense of possibility and optimism.

Non-Verbal Communication: What You Say Without Words

Non-verbal cues are powerful. They can either reinforce your message or create doubts in the listener's mind. Mastering body language, eye contact, and other non-verbal signals will elevate your communication game.

Maintain Open Body Language

Crossed arms, slouched shoulders, or looking distracted can signal disinterest or insecurity. Instead, stand or sit upright, keep your arms relaxed, and face the person you're speaking to. Open body language invites trust and connection.

Make Eye Contact

Looking someone in the eyes conveys honesty and attentiveness. It doesn't mean staring uncomfortably, but maintaining natural eye contact shows that you're engaged and confident.

Mirror the Customer's Energy

People tend to connect with those who match their energy levels. If a customer is upbeat and animated, mirror that enthusiasm. If they're more reserved, adopt a calm and steady tone. This creates rapport and helps them feel at ease.

Active Listening: The Key to Understanding

Effective communication isn't just about talking—it's about listening. Active listening allows you to truly understand your customer's needs, concerns, and goals.

How to Listen Actively

1. **Focus Fully**: Eliminate distractions and give your undivided attention. Put your phone away and be present.

2. **Acknowledge Their Words**: Nodding, maintaining eye contact, and using phrases like "I understand" or "Tell me more" show that you're engaged.

3. **Pause Before Responding**: Resist the urge to jump in with a solution. Sometimes, customers reveal deeper concerns if you let them finish their thought.

Listen Between the Lines

Sometimes, what a customer doesn't say is as important as what they do. Pay attention to their tone, hesitations, and body language. These can provide clues about their true feelings or unspoken objections.

Asking the Right Questions

Great communicators know how to ask questions that guide the conversation and uncover valuable insights.

Types of Questions to Master

- **Open-Ended Questions**: Encourage dialogue and detailed responses. For example, "What's been your biggest challenge in this area?"

- **Clarifying Questions**: Ensure you understand their needs fully. For example, "When you say convenience is important, what does that look like for you?"

- **Leading Questions**: Subtly direct the conversation toward your product's benefits. For example, "Wouldn't it be helpful if you had a solution that saved you time and effort?"

Follow-Up Questions

Don't stop at surface-level answers. Dig deeper by asking follow-ups like, "Why is that important to you?" or "How has that impacted your business so far?"

Guiding the Conversation Toward Closing

Every effective sales conversation has a natural progression: building rapport, identifying needs, presenting solutions, and addressing objections. The key is to guide this journey seamlessly through your communication.

Transitioning Naturally

Once you've identified the customer's needs, use smooth transitions to introduce your product. For example, "Based on what you've shared, I think this could be a great fit for you. Let me explain how it works."

Handling Objections with Empathy

When objections arise, don't get defensive. Acknowledge their concern, empathize, and address it with a solution. For example, "I understand that cost is a concern. Let's look at how this investment could save you money in the long run."

Practicing Communication Skills

Like any skill, mastering communication takes practice. Role-play conversations with a colleague, record yourself to analyze your tone and delivery, and seek feedback from others. Over time, these efforts will refine your ability to speak with purpose and confidence.

Bringing It All Together

Effective communication is about more than just delivering a message—it's about connecting, listening, and responding with intention. When you speak with purpose and authenticity, you create conversations that build trust, solve problems, and ultimately lead to success.

So, go out there and practice. Every conversation is an opportunity to refine your craft and strengthen your relationships. Remember: the best communicators don't just sell—they inspire.

Chapter 5:

Overcoming Objections – Turning "No" into "Yes"

Objections are as natural to the sales process as conversations. When a customer raises an objection, it doesn't mean the sale is lost—it means they're engaging with you. Objections are opportunities to clarify, connect, and ultimately guide your customer toward a solution that works for them.

Mastering the art of handling objections is a critical skill for every saleswoman. It's about listening, empathizing, and providing answers that turn doubts into trust. This chapter will equip you with strategies to confidently tackle objections and turn "no" into "yes" with grace and professionalism.

The Role of Objections in Sales

Objections aren't rejections—they're requests for more information. When a customer voices a concern, it's often because they need reassurance, a deeper understanding, or a solution to a perceived barrier.

Instead of seeing objections as barriers, view them as windows into the customer's thought process. A well-addressed objection can strengthen your relationship and make the sale even more meaningful.

Common Types of Objections and How to Address Them

1. Price Objections: "It's Too Expensive"

Price concerns are among the most common objections. Instead of immediately lowering your price, focus on highlighting the value of your product.

Strategy:

- **Acknowledge the Concern**: "I understand that price is an important factor."
- **Shift to Value**: "Let's talk about how this investment can save you time and money in the long run."
- **Provide Perspective**: Break down the cost into smaller, more manageable terms. For example, "When you look at it as just $3 a day, it's more affordable than your daily coffee."

2. Timing Objections: "I Need to Think About It"

Sometimes, customers hesitate because they're unsure or not ready to commit.

Strategy:

- **Show Understanding**: "I completely understand that you want to take some time to think it over."

- **Ask Questions**: "What specific concerns do you have that I can help address right now?"

- **Create Urgency**: If appropriate, highlight limited-time offers or the cost of waiting: "This deal is only available this week, and I'd hate for you to miss out."

3. Trust Objections: "I'm Not Sure This Will Work for Me"

When trust is the issue, your job is to build credibility and demonstrate the product's reliability.

Strategy:

- **Empathize**: "I understand why you might feel unsure—making the right choice is important."

- **Share Testimonials**: Offer real-life success stories or data to back up your claims.
- **Provide Guarantees**: "We're so confident in this product that we offer a money-back guarantee if it doesn't meet your expectations."

4. Competitor Objections: "I'm Already Using Something Similar"

If a customer mentions a competitor, it's an opportunity to showcase what sets you apart.

Strategy:

- **Acknowledge the Competition**: "It sounds like you've done your research, which is great!"
- **Differentiate Your Offer**: Highlight unique features, superior service, or better results.

- **Ask About Satisfaction**: "How has your experience been with that product? What do you feel it's missing?"

The 3-Step Formula for Handling Objections

When faced with an objection, use this three-step approach to respond effectively:

1. **Listen Without Interrupting**

    Let the customer finish their thought completely. Interrupting can make them feel unheard or dismissed.

2. **Acknowledge and Empathize**

    Show the customer that their concern is valid. For example, "I can see why you might feel that way." This builds trust and opens the door for further dialogue.

3. **Respond with Solutions**

Once you've acknowledged their concern, provide a clear and tailored response that addresses the objection head-on.

Turning Objections into Opportunities

Reframe the Objection

An objection can be an opening to highlight a product's strengths. For example, if a customer says, "This seems complicated," you can respond, "That's a great point. The reason it looks detailed is that it's designed to handle all aspects of your needs efficiently."

Ask Open-Ended Questions

Encourage the customer to elaborate on their concerns. Open-ended questions help you gather more information to tailor your response. For example:

- "What specifically makes you feel this isn't the right fit?"
- "Can you tell me more about what you're looking for?"

Involve the Customer in the Solution

Instead of dictating a solution, involve the customer in the process. For example:

- "What would make this product feel like a better fit for you?"

Maintaining Grace Under Pressure

Handling objections requires emotional intelligence. Stay calm, patient, and composed, even if the customer's tone feels challenging. Avoid taking objections personally—they're about the product or process, not you.

If you feel the conversation is getting stuck, don't be afraid to take a step back. Offer to follow up later: "I can see this is a big decision. How about I give you some time to think, and I'll check back with you next week?"

Turning "No" into a Future "Yes"

Not every objection will lead to an immediate sale, and that's okay. Sometimes, a "no" today can turn into a "yes" later.

Follow-Up Matters

Stay in touch with potential customers after they've raised objections. Send them helpful resources, updates, or a simple check-in to show that you care about their needs beyond the sale.

Build Long-Term Relationships

Even if you don't close the deal now, a well-handled objection can leave a positive impression, making the customer more likely to consider you in the future.

Embrace Objections with Confidence

Objections are not the end of the sales process—they're pivotal moments where trust is built, relationships are strengthened, and solutions are solidified.

By mastering the art of addressing objections, you'll not only improve your ability to close sales but also grow as a confident, solutions-oriented saleswoman. Remember, every objection is an opportunity in disguise—embrace it, address it, and watch the magic happen.

Chapter 6:

Closing the Deal – Sealing the Sale with Confidence

Closing the deal. It's the moment every salesperson works towards, and yet, it's often the most intimidating part of the sales process. The truth is, closing isn't about pressuring the customer into making a decision they're not ready for. It's about guiding the conversation toward a natural conclusion where both parties are satisfied. When done correctly, closing the sale feels like the next logical step in a relationship, not an aggressive tactic.

In this chapter, we'll explore the art of closing with confidence, providing you with proven techniques and strategies to seal the deal every time. Whether you're talking to a first-time buyer or a long-time client, mastering the close is essential to your success.

You don't need to be pushy or salesy—you just need to be clear, confident, and know how to recognize when the time is right.

Understanding the Close: More Than Just a Transaction

Before diving into specific techniques, it's important to understand that closing the deal isn't just about finalizing the transaction. It's about creating an experience that resonates with the customer. When you close a sale, you are solidifying the trust you've built throughout the conversation, and you're confirming that what you're offering is the right solution for their needs.

A good close is about recognizing when the customer is ready to commit and guiding them toward making a decision they feel confident about. It's not about manipulation or pressure; it's about helping them make the best decision, both for themselves and for your business.

The Key Elements of Closing

1. **Timing**

    Timing is everything when it comes to closing. You need to be able to read the conversation and recognize the signs that a customer is ready to make a commitment. If you're too early, you might risk pushing them away. If you're too late, they may lose interest.

Signs that it's time to close:

- The customer starts asking logistical questions like, "When can I get this delivered?" or "How does the payment process work?"
- They express interest in specific features or benefits that directly align with their needs.
- They start imagining themselves using the product or service, often speaking in terms like, "This would really help me with..." or "I can see how this will solve my problem."

2. **Confidence**

Confidence is contagious. When you speak confidently about your product and its benefits, your customer will be more inclined to trust you and feel comfortable making the decision. Confidence comes from knowing your product inside and out, and it comes from understanding the value you're offering.

If you don't believe in your product, neither will the customer. On the other hand, if you approach the close with a clear belief in what you're offering and its ability to solve the customer's problem, your confidence will inspire theirs. Remember: you're not just selling a product—you're offering a solution.

3. **Clarity**

   Clear communication is critical when closing the deal. This means being direct but respectful in guiding the customer toward a decision. Avoid using vague or complicated language. Be clear about the next steps, the pricing, and the benefits of taking action now. The more straightforward you are, the more comfortable the customer will feel.

Closing Techniques You Can Use

Now let's explore the different closing techniques that will help you confidently seal the deal.

1. The Direct Close

This is the simplest and most straightforward closing technique. After addressing all the customer's concerns, you ask for the sale directly. While it's a simple approach, it can be highly effective when you've already built rapport and established trust.

Example:

- "It sounds like this is exactly what you're looking for. Would you like to go ahead and place your order today?"

While it may seem blunt, this approach works because it demonstrates confidence and helps the customer make a decision. If they're ready, they'll appreciate your straightforwardness. If they need more time, they'll likely give you their reasoning, allowing you to address any last concerns.

2. The Assumptive Close

The assumptive close is based on the idea that the customer has already mentally committed to the purchase. You guide the conversation by assuming they're ready to move forward.

Example:

- "Great, let's get this started. What's the best address for delivery?"

This technique works because it projects confidence and assumes the decision has already been made. The key here is ensuring that you've done enough groundwork during your previous conversations to make the customer feel comfortable enough to say "yes." You're not forcing them to make a decision, but rather facilitating the natural next step in the process.

3. The Urgency Close

Sometimes, customers need a little nudge to take action. By adding a sense of urgency, you encourage them to make a decision sooner rather than later. This could be because of a time-sensitive offer, a limited quantity, or the fear of missing out on a special opportunity.

Example:

- "Just so you know, we only have a few items left at this price, and I wouldn't want you to miss out."

This technique works when you have a genuine reason to create urgency. If your product or service is truly in limited supply, or if there's a limited-time offer, make sure you communicate that in a way that motivates action. But be careful—creating false urgency can backfire and damage your relationship with the customer if they find out it's not true.

4. The Summary Close

This approach involves summarizing the key benefits of the product or service that align with the customer's needs and desires. You're essentially recapping everything that led the customer to this point, which can reinforce their decision and give them the final nudge toward a "yes."

Example:

- "So, just to recap, this product will help you save time, it's easy to use, and it comes with a 30-day satisfaction guarantee. Based on everything we've discussed, I think it's the perfect solution for you. Are you ready to move forward today?"

The Summary Close reinforces the value you've already established and leaves no room for doubt about why this is the right decision.

5. The Question Close

The question is all about asking a question that leads the customer to confirm their desire to purchase. This could be a direct question or a question that prompts them to think more deeply about the product and its benefits.

Example:

- "How soon would you like to get started with this solution?"

By posing a question that focuses on their readiness or excitement to begin using the product, you make them feel more engaged and help them take the final step.

Handling Last-Minute Objections

Even when you've done everything right, there may be one last objection that pops up just before the close. This is normal, and it doesn't mean the sale is lost. Instead of getting discouraged, use this as a final opportunity to address the concern and reassure the customer.

Be Prepared with Solutions

It's helpful to anticipate common last-minute objections and have a solution ready. Whether it's a question about payment options, shipping times, or product details, make sure you have the information ready to resolve any final hesitations.

When to Walk Away

Not every customer is going to be the right fit for your product or service. If it becomes clear that a customer isn't ready to buy or doesn't truly need what you're offering, don't be afraid to walk away. It's important to recognize when the timing just isn't right.

Leaving the door open for future conversations is key. Politely acknowledge their decision and let them know you're available if they change their mind.

Closing the deal doesn't have to be stressful or intimidating. By understanding the different closing techniques and recognizing when the time is right, you can approach the final step with confidence. The key is to provide value, build trust, and guide the customer toward a decision that's in their best interest. When you close with clarity, confidence, and purpose, you'll seal the deal every time.

Chapter 7:

The Power of Follow-Up – Keep the Conversation Alive

Sales don't end with a signature, a handshake, or the exchange of money. These actions represent just the beginning of a relationship—one that can lead to repeat business, customer loyalty, and a strong network of advocates for your brand. The follow-up is one of the most powerful tools in your sales arsenal. It's an essential step in not just closing the deal, but in ensuring that your customers stay satisfied, engaged, and connected to your brand long after the sale is made.

In this chapter, we'll delve into the critical importance of the follow-up and explore how you can leverage it to turn one-time customers into loyal, long-term clients. You'll learn how to keep the conversation alive, nurture relationships, address concerns, and create a customer experience that leads to repeat business and referrals.

Why Follow-Up Matters

In today's world, where competition is fierce and attention spans are short, your initial sale might not be enough to guarantee future business. Customers have options, and they're not afraid to look elsewhere if they feel ignored or undervalued. This is where follow-up comes into play. By checking in with your customers, you demonstrate that you care about more than just making the sale—you care about their experience, satisfaction, and success.

Here's why follow-up matters:

1. **Customer Retention**

    The cost of acquiring a new customer is

significantly higher than the cost of retaining an existing one. By following up, you increase the likelihood of repeat business, which is far more profitable in the long term. A happy customer is more likely to return for additional purchases, sign up for new services, or refer you to others.

2. **Build Trust**

A follow-up is a signal to the customer that you're invested in the relationship, not just the transaction. When customers feel that you genuinely care about their experience, they are more likely to trust you and see you as a reliable source. This trust is essential in building lasting relationships.

3. **Generate Referrals**

   Satisfied customers are often more than willing to recommend your services to others, but they need to feel valued first. A thoughtful follow-up can prompt your customers to spread the word about your business, creating an organic stream of referrals that can grow your clientele base.

4. **Increase Upsell and Cross-Sell Opportunities**

   The follow-up offers a unique opportunity to learn more about your customer's evolving needs. By maintaining an open line of communication, you can introduce them to new products or services that complement their original purchase, increasing the value of each customer over time.

When to Follow Up

Knowing when to follow up is just as important as the act itself. Too soon, and you risk coming across as pushy; too late, and you might miss the opportunity to resolve concerns or capitalize on additional sales.

Timing your follow-up is essential for maximizing its effectiveness. Here's a general guide on when to reach out to your customers:

1. **Immediately After the Sale**

    Your first follow-up should happen shortly after the transaction. This is the perfect time to express your gratitude, confirm their purchase, and ensure everything is running smoothly. The goal here is to reinforce their decision and begin building rapport for the long term.

Example:

- "Thank you for choosing [product/service]. We hope you're enjoying it so far. If you have any questions or need assistance, don't hesitate to reach out. We're here to help!"

2. **Within 24 to 48 Hours**

    A second follow-up within the first 1-2 days is a great time to check in and ensure the customer's satisfaction. This is an opportunity to ask if they have any immediate concerns or if they need any guidance on using the product or service. It also shows that you're committed to their experience, not just the sale.

Example:

- "I wanted to follow up and see how everything is going with your new [product]. Is there anything we can assist you with to ensure you're getting the most out of it?"

3. **One Week Later**

   A follow-up about a week after the sale is an ideal time to ask for feedback and provide additional support if needed. You can ask how the product is fitting into their routine, and if they've encountered any challenges. This is also an excellent opportunity to ask for a testimonial or review, should they be happy with their purchase.

Example:

- "How has the [product] been working for you? Your feedback is valuable, and we'd love to hear about your experience so far. If there's anything we can do to make it even better, please let us know!"

4. **One Month Later**

    At this point, you've given your customer time to fully experience the product. Now is the time to check in again to ensure it's still meeting their needs, and to introduce new products or services they might be interested in based on their original purchase.

Example:

- "It's been about a month since your purchase, and we wanted to check in and see how things are going. Are there any other areas where we can assist or offer solutions that might enhance your experience?"

How to Follow Up Effectively

Successful follow-up doesn't mean bombarding your customers with emails, calls, or messages. It's about creating a balance between staying present without overwhelming them. Below are a few best practices for effective follow-up:

1. Personalize Your Communication

A follow-up email or message should never feel like a generic template. Personalizing your communication makes the customer feel valued and shows that you're paying attention to their needs. Reference the specific product or service they purchased and, if possible, mention previous conversations to demonstrate that you remember them.

Example:

- "Hi [Customer Name], I hope you're enjoying the [product] we discussed last week. I wanted to follow up and ensure you've been able to get the most out of it. Let me know if you have any questions or need any further assistance."

2. Use Multiple Channels

Not all customers prefer the same method of communication. While one person may respond best to an email, another may appreciate a quick text message or a phone call. Offering various channels for follow-up gives your customers flexibility and ensures that you're reaching them in the way they prefer.

3. Be Solution-Oriented

Don't make your follow-up about you. Focus on providing value to the customer by offering solutions to any problems they might be encountering. By keeping the focus on their experience, you reinforce your commitment to helping them succeed.

Example:

- "We noticed you mentioned having difficulty with [feature]. We have a few tips and resources that could help you make the most of it. Would you like me to send those over?"

4. Show Gratitude

A little appreciation goes a long way. Be sure to thank your customers for their time, their business, and their feedback. People love to feel appreciated, and a genuine thank you can foster a positive relationship that encourages repeat business.

What to Do After the Follow-Up

After you've made your follow-up, don't simply leave things hanging. Take action on any feedback you've received and continue to nurture the relationship.

- **If they're satisfied**: Thank them and let them know you're available for any future needs. This is also a good time to ask for a referral or review.

- **If they have concerns**: Address them promptly and professionally. Use this as an opportunity to showcase your commitment to customer satisfaction. Offer solutions and assure them that you're there to support them long-term.

- **If they don't respond**: Don't take it personally. Customers can be busy, or they may not be ready for another purchase. Try a gentle follow-up after a couple of weeks, reminding them of your services and asking if there's anything new you can help them with.

The power of follow-up lies in your ability to build lasting relationships that extend beyond the initial transaction. It's about continuing the conversation, ensuring satisfaction, and demonstrating that your value to the customer isn't limited to the sale itself. By mastering the art of follow-up, you'll foster customer loyalty, increase your chances of repeat business, and position yourself as a trusted advisor who truly cares about your customers' success.

Sales don't end when the deal is done—they only just begun. And with the right follow-up strategy, you can ensure that the connection stays strong, and the opportunity for future growth is always there. Keep the conversation alive, and watch your business thrive.

Chapter 8:

Selling with Integrity – Build Trust and Reputation

In the world of sales, the focus often falls on closing deals, hitting targets, and driving revenue. But these short-term goals can only take you so far if you don't build the foundational element of any successful career: trust. Trust is the cornerstone of long-term success, and it's something that can't be bought, rushed, or manipulated. It must be earned, consistently, over time, through integrity.

Selling with integrity doesn't just mean doing the right thing when it's easy—it means doing the right thing, even when no one is watching, and even when it might cost you a sale. It's about treating your customers fairly, honestly, and respectfully, and offering solutions that truly benefit them, not just your bottom line. This chapter is dedicated to teaching you how to sell with integrity, ensuring that you build a reputation that attracts loyal clients, generates repeat business, and makes you a trusted resource in your field.

What Does Selling with Integrity Really Mean?

Integrity is often misunderstood or overlooked in the fast-paced world of sales. In many sales environments, success can be measured by the number of deals closed or the revenue generated. But the true measure of success in sales should be how well you build relationships, help your clients achieve their goals, and represent your values in everything you do.

Selling with integrity means:

- **Honesty**: Being truthful with your customers about your product or service, including its limitations. You should never oversell, misrepresent, or deceive in an effort to make a sale. Customers appreciate transparency, and they will trust you more when you provide them with realistic expectations.

- **Respect**: Valuing your customers as individuals, not just as potential sales. This means listening actively, understanding their needs, and treating them with kindness and courtesy, regardless of whether or not they make a purchase.

- **Accountability**: Taking responsibility for both the good and the bad. If something goes wrong, owning up to it and taking the steps necessary to make it right. This includes handling complaints gracefully and addressing customer concerns promptly and professionally.

- **Authenticity**: Being yourself and letting your true personality shine through in your interactions. Customers can tell when you're being authentic, and they will appreciate the sincerity you bring to the table.

- **Long-term Focus**: Recognizing that each sale is part of a bigger picture. Instead of focusing on one-time profits, integrity-driven salespeople focus on creating lasting relationships that bring ongoing value to both the customer and the salesperson.

Why Integrity is Non-Negotiable in Sales

The long-term benefits of selling with integrity far outweigh any short-term gains that may come from cutting corners or taking shortcuts. Here's why integrity is crucial:

1. **Trust Leads to Repeat Business**

    When customers trust you, they're more likely to come back to you for future needs. They know that you'll provide them with honest advice, that your products or services will meet their needs, and that you will follow through on your promises. Trust creates loyalty, and loyal customers are the foundation of a successful sales career.

2. **Referrals Come from Trust**

Satisfied customers who trust you are more likely to refer you to their friends, family, and colleagues. Referrals are one of the most effective ways to grow your client base, and they almost always come from customers who feel they've been treated fairly and with respect.

3. **Enhanced Reputation**

Your reputation is everything in sales. A salesperson with integrity builds a reputation as someone who can be trusted, who provides value, and who puts the customer's best interests first. Word spreads fast, and customers will seek you out because they know that you represent quality, honesty, and reliability.

4. **Higher Job Satisfaction**

Selling with integrity allows you to feel good about the work you're doing. You can go home each night knowing that you didn't compromise your values or take advantage of anyone. This leads to higher job satisfaction and a greater sense of pride in your work.

5. **Long-Term Success**

While a "quick win" might bring short-term financial rewards, the long-term success that comes from selling with integrity is far more fulfilling and sustainable. Integrity-based sales create steady growth, a loyal client base, and a strong reputation—ingredients that are essential for lasting success.

How to Sell with Integrity: Key Strategies

Now that we understand why integrity is vital to long-term success in sales, let's explore practical strategies for building and maintaining it in your daily sales interactions.

1. Be Honest About Your Product or Service

One of the easiest ways to sell with integrity is to be honest about what you're selling. This means acknowledging both the strengths and limitations of your product or service. Never promise something that your product can't deliver, and always be upfront about any potential drawbacks.

Example:

Instead of saying, "This product will solve all your problems," say, "This product addresses these key challenges, but it may not be the best fit for everything you need. Let's look at alternatives to make sure we find the right solution for you."

This transparency builds trust and shows that you have the customer's best interests at heart.

2. Listen to Understand, Not Just to Sell

Listening is the foundation of any good sales conversation. But listening with integrity means actively trying to understand your customer's needs and goals, rather than simply waiting for your chance to pitch your product.

Ask open-ended questions, probe for deeper insights, and ensure that you understand the pain points that your product or service can solve. By truly listening, you can recommend the best solutions, which will naturally lead to a more successful and respectful sales process.

Example:

Instead of jumping straight into your pitch, ask, "Can you tell me more about the challenges you're facing right now?" By understanding the problem before suggesting a solution, you're showing that you care more about their needs than making a sale.

3. Put the Customer's Interests First

Selling with integrity means that your focus is on helping the customer, not just meeting your sales quota. Put the customer's needs above the immediate sale, and be willing to walk away if what you're offering isn't the right fit for them.

For example, if you're selling a product or service that's not a good match for a customer, don't try to make the sale anyway. Instead, recommend alternatives or guide them toward a solution that better fits their needs—even if it means losing the sale. Customers will appreciate your honesty and will trust you in the long run.

Example:

"If this product doesn't address your needs, I'd be happy to recommend something else, even if it means you'll need to look elsewhere for the time being."

4. Follow Through on Promises

If you make a promise to a customer, whether it's about delivery times, product functionality, or follow-up actions, you must deliver on that promise. Integrity in sales is about being reliable and consistent. If you say you'll do something, do it. If circumstances change, communicate that honestly with the customer and offer a solution.

Example:

If you promise to send more information after a meeting, follow up promptly. If there's a delay in delivery, inform the customer ahead of time rather than leaving them to wonder what's going on.

5. Accept Accountability for Mistakes

No one is perfect, and mistakes can happen in any sales process. If you make an error, own up to it immediately and work to resolve it. Handling mistakes with integrity shows that you take responsibility for your actions and that you value the customer's experience.

Example:

"If there's a problem with your order, I apologize. Let's work together to get this resolved as quickly as possible. I'll make sure we find a solution that works for you."

By taking ownership of the issue, you demonstrate to the customer that their satisfaction is your priority.

Building Your Reputation Through Integrity

Your reputation is built over time through consistent actions and behaviors that demonstrate integrity. In the sales world, word-of-mouth is incredibly powerful. The more customers trust you, the more likely they are to refer you to others, share their positive experiences, and come back for future purchases.

Integrity allows you to build a reputation as someone who can be counted on—someone who doesn't just push products but who offers real value and support. Your reputation will precede you, and soon you won't have to chase clients; they will come to you because they know that you operate with honesty and respect.

Trust is the Key to Lasting Success

Selling with integrity isn't just a moral choice—it's a business strategy. It leads to repeat business, referrals, and a stellar reputation that will carry you through the ups and downs of your sales career. When you prioritize honesty, transparency, and accountability, you create strong, lasting relationships with your customers. And in the end, those relationships are what will drive your long-term success.

By selling with integrity, you build not just a customer base but a foundation of trust and respect that will sustain you for years to come. So, remember: being a successful salesperson isn't just about hitting targets. It's about maintaining integrity, building trust, and ensuring that your reputation is your strongest asset.

Chapter 9:

Setting and Achieving Sales Goals – Stay Focused and Driven

In sales, the one thing that separates top performers from the rest is the ability to set clear, achievable goals. Whether you're just starting out or you're a seasoned pro, having specific goals in place is critical. Without them, it's easy to lose focus, get sidetracked, or simply feel stuck. But with the right goals, you not only know where you're going but also have the motivation to keep going, even when things get tough.

This chapter will guide you through the process of setting goals that not only motivate you but are achievable and measurable. You'll learn how to break down big goals into small, actionable steps, track your progress, and stay on course when obstacles come your way. Whether you're trying to hit a monthly sales target, grow your client base, or become a top producer, mastering goal-setting is key to a successful career in sales.

Why Clear, Achievable Goals Matter

In any field, but especially in sales, clear goals are your roadmap. Without them, you're essentially wandering around without direction. With them, you know exactly where you're headed, and you can chart a path to get there. Goals give you purpose, clarity, and a sense of progress, all of which keep you on track.

So, why are goals so powerful?

1. **Clarity**: Having a goal means you know what you're working toward. Without a goal, you might get distracted by day-to-day tasks that don't move you forward. When you know your

goal, you can make every action count.

2. **Motivation**: Sales is tough. There will be days when you get more "no's" than "yes's," and motivation can be hard to find. But a clear goal acts like a compass, helping you push through the tough times and stay motivated because you're working toward something meaningful.

3. **Measurability**: Goals allow you to track your progress. Whether you're aiming to hit a certain sales number, grow your network, or become the top performer on your team, having a measurable goal makes it easy to see how far you've come—and how far you still need to go.

4. **Direction**: A clear goal gives you a sense of direction. It's like having a GPS for your career. You'll know exactly what steps to take and when, helping you stay focused and organized.

Without goals, you're just floating through your sales career. But when you set specific, clear goals, you're driving toward success with purpose.

Breaking Goals Into Manageable Steps

Now that you know why goals are so important, let's talk about how to break them down into manageable steps. Big goals can be overwhelming, especially in sales where pressure can feel relentless. But the key to achieving anything big is taking it one step at a time.

For example, let's say your goal is to close 10 deals in a month. Instead of fixating on that big number, break it down into smaller, more achievable targets. How many deals do you need to close each week? What actions do you need to take to make it happen?

Here's how you break down your goals into smaller, actionable steps:

1. **Start with the Big Goal**: What is your main goal? Maybe it's hitting your monthly sales target, closing a specific number of deals, or getting a certain number of meetings. Start big, then zoom in on how to get there.

2. **Set Milestones**: Break the big goal into smaller checkpoints. For instance, if your goal is to close 10 deals, you could aim to close 2 or 3 deals per week. It makes it feel less overwhelming and

keeps you focused.

3. **Define Specific Actions**: What do you need to do to hit those milestones? Maybe it's prospecting new leads, following up with existing clients, or scheduling demos. Breaking down each task into specifics helps you stay organized and makes your goal feel more achievable.

4. **Make it S.M.A.R.T.**: Apply the SMART goal framework to make sure your goals are Specific, Measurable, Achievable, Relevant, and Time-bound. Instead of just saying "I want to make more sales," say something like "I want to close 10 deals by the end of the month by

following up with 5 leads each week and scheduling 3 demos per week."

Tracking Progress and Adjusting Your Approach

Tracking your progress is one of the most important aspects of goal-setting. Without it, it's hard to know if you're on the right track. It also helps you identify any adjustments you might need to make along the way.

Here are some ways to track your progress:

1. **Daily Check-ins**: At the end of each day, reflect on what you've accomplished. Did you hit your call or meeting goals? Did you close any deals? Did you learn anything valuable from your interactions? Tracking your daily wins, no matter how small, helps you stay motivated.

2. **Weekly and Monthly Reviews**: In addition to daily check-ins, schedule time each week or month to assess how close you are to hitting your big goal. Are you on track? If not, figure out why and adjust your plan. Periodic reviews help you stay on top of things and avoid falling behind.

3. **Use Tools**: Use a CRM, sales tracker, or even a simple spreadsheet to monitor your progress. Visualizing your sales numbers can be incredibly motivating. Plus, it gives you a clear picture of where you're excelling and where you need to focus more attention.

4. **Adjust When Needed**: Sometimes things don't go as planned. The sales cycle might be slower

than expected, or external factors might cause a delay. That's fine. The important thing is to be flexible and adjust your approach as needed. If something isn't working, try a different tactic.

Staying Accountable

Accountability is key to staying motivated and on track to meet your goals. It's easy to lose focus without someone holding you accountable, and self-motivation can sometimes fall short. Here's how to stay accountable:

1. **Set Deadlines**: Deadlines are powerful motivators. If you have a clear timeline for when you want to achieve your goal, you'll feel the urgency to keep pushing. Break down your larger goal into smaller chunks with deadlines

for each, and you'll have a clear path forward.

2. **Find an Accountability Partner**: Whether it's a friend, colleague, or mentor, having someone check in on your progress helps keep you on track. They don't have to micromanage you, but simply checking in from time to time makes you feel more responsible for your actions.

3. **Track Your Daily Habits**: Identify the key habits that will drive your success—like making a certain number of calls or scheduling demos—and track them daily. This keeps you on track and ensures you're doing the work needed to hit your targets.

4. **Celebrate Wins**: Recognize the progress you make. When you hit a milestone, take a moment to celebrate it. Big wins don't happen without small wins along the way, so acknowledging these victories helps you stay motivated.

The Right Mindset for Achieving Your Goals

Your mindset plays a huge role in whether or not you achieve your goals. Having a growth mindset—the belief that you can improve and grow through effort—helps you push through the tough moments and stay on course. Sales will always have its ups and downs, but how you handle them determines your success.

Here's how to keep a positive, goal-oriented mindset:

1. **Visualize Success**: Take time each day to imagine what success looks like. Picture yourself hitting your sales target, closing deals, and achieving the recognition you want. Visualization helps reinforce your belief that your goals are achievable.

2. **Stay Resilient**: Sales is full of rejections, setbacks, and challenges. It's important to remain resilient. Learn to see setbacks as opportunities to learn and grow, not as failures. Every "no" brings you one step closer to a "yes."

3. **Focus on Progress, Not Perfection**: Perfectionism can be paralyzing. Don't get hung up on doing everything perfectly. Instead, focus on making progress. As long as you're moving

forward and improving, you're on the right path.

Achieving Your Sales Goals

Sales is a journey, and achieving your goals takes time, effort, and perseverance. By setting clear, achievable goals, breaking them down into manageable steps, tracking your progress, and holding yourself accountable, you create a roadmap to success. Stay focused, stay driven, and remember that every step you take brings you closer to your goal.

Success in sales doesn't happen overnight, but with the right mindset, plan, and consistency, you will reach your targets and become a top performer. So get started today—set your goals, take action, and keep pushing. Your success is waiting for you.

Chapter 10:

Celebrate Your Success – Reflect, Recharge, and Keep Growing

In sales, it's easy to get caught up in the hustle. The constant push to close the next deal, hit the next target, or reach the next milestone can sometimes make us forget to pause and appreciate how far we've come. Success isn't just about the numbers—it's also about the journey, the growth, and the victories, big and small, that got you here. This chapter is all about celebrating your wins, reflecting on your progress, recharging your energy, and setting yourself up for continued success in the fast-paced world of sales.

Whether you've closed a big deal, hit a new sales record, or simply exceeded your goals for the week, it's essential to take a moment to acknowledge and celebrate your success. But celebration doesn't stop with a pat on the back. It's about reflection, learning, and using what you've accomplished to fuel your next big step. This chapter will explore why celebrating success is vital, how to recharge and refocus, and how to keep growing and evolving in your sales career.

The Power of Celebration: Why It Matters

It's easy to fall into the trap of thinking that success is just a stepping stone to the next goal. But without celebrating your achievements, you miss the opportunity to fully recognize and enjoy the fruits of your labor. Success is about progress, and progress should be celebrated.

Why celebrate?

1. **Acknowledging Your Hard Work**: Every deal closed, every new lead converted, and every target hit is the result of hard work, dedication, and perseverance. Celebrating these moments helps reinforce the fact that your efforts matter, and it motivates you to continue striving toward your next goal.

2. **Building Confidence**: Success, whether big or small, is proof that you're capable. Celebrating your wins boosts your confidence, reminding you that you have what it takes to succeed. It strengthens your belief in yourself and your ability to close deals, grow relationships, and overcome challenges.

3. **Staying Motivated**: Sales is a challenging career, and staying motivated can be tough. Celebrating your wins keeps you energized. Each success serves as fuel for your next goal. The positive reinforcement from recognizing your achievements creates momentum that propels you forward.

4. **Creating a Positive Mindset**: Sales is filled with highs and lows. Sometimes, it can feel like a constant grind. Celebrating your success, no matter how small, helps you keep a positive outlook. It reminds you of what you've accomplished, even when you're facing setbacks or rejections.

Reflecting on Your Journey: Learning from Your Wins and Challenges

Celebration isn't just about the good times—it's also about reflection. Looking back on your journey gives you the opportunity to assess what's worked, what hasn't, and how far you've come. Reflection allows you to understand your strengths, identify areas for improvement, and prepare for future success.

Take time to look back on the deals you've closed, the relationships you've built, and the challenges you've faced. What did you do right? What could you have done differently? Reflecting on both the wins and the setbacks gives you valuable insights into your growth and development as a salesperson.

1. **Analyze Your Successes**: When you achieve a goal or close a deal, ask yourself what

contributed to that success. Was it a particular strategy or approach that worked well? Did you build rapport in a specific way that resonated with your customer? Understanding what led to your success helps you replicate those actions in the future.

2. **Learn from Your Challenges**: Not every deal will close, and not every day will be a win. It's important to look at setbacks as opportunities to learn. What went wrong? Was there something you could have done differently? Maybe you missed an opportunity to build rapport or didn't follow up as effectively as you could have. The key is to learn from those moments and use them as stepping stones for improvement.

3. **Identify Your Strengths**: Reflecting on your journey also allows you to see where you've excelled. Are you particularly skilled at building relationships? Do you have a knack for uncovering customer pain points? Recognizing your strengths enables you to continue honing those skills and bring them to the forefront in future sales conversations.

4. **Set New Goals**: After reflecting on your progress, set new goals for yourself. Sales is an ever-evolving field, and your goals should grow along with you. Whether you're aiming to close more deals, improve your conversion rates, or build stronger relationships with your clients, setting new goals keeps you focused and motivated.

Recharging: Staying Energized for the Long Haul

Sales can be exhausting. Between the constant pressure to meet targets, the long hours of prospecting, and the emotional rollercoaster of rejection and success, it's easy to burn out. This is why taking time to recharge is just as important as celebrating your success. If you don't take care of yourself, your sales performance will suffer.

1. **Take Time for Yourself**: Schedule time to step away from the grind. Whether it's a weekend getaway, an afternoon off, or simply taking a few hours to unwind, giving yourself permission to recharge is essential. Sales is a marathon, not a sprint, and taking time to rest helps you

maintain the stamina needed to keep going.

2. **Find Balance**: While sales is important, your well-being comes first. Finding a balance between work and personal life is key to staying energized and motivated. Take care of your physical health, mental well-being, and relationships outside of work. The healthier and happier you are, the better you'll perform in your sales career.

3. **Reconnect with Your Purpose**: Sometimes, when the grind gets tough, it's easy to forget why you started in the first place. Take time to reconnect with your "why." Whether it's the desire to help people, the ambition to build a successful career, or the dream of achieving

financial freedom, remembering your purpose reignites your passion and motivation.

Keep Growing: The Sales World Never Stops Evolving

The world of sales is constantly changing. New technologies, evolving customer expectations, and fresh approaches to selling mean that no one can afford to rest on their laurels. To stay ahead, you must always be learning and growing.

1. **Embrace Continuous Learning**: Sales is a dynamic field, and the best salespeople are those who are always learning. Attend webinars, read books, listen to podcasts, and stay informed about the latest trends in sales. The more you learn, the more equipped you'll be to

navigate the ever-changing landscape of sales.

2. **Develop New Skills**: In addition to keeping up with industry trends, focus on developing new skills. Maybe you need to improve your negotiation skills, become more proficient in using CRM tools, or learn how to manage your time more effectively. The more well-rounded you are, the better you'll be at handling any sales situation that comes your way.

3. **Seek Feedback**: Don't just rely on self-reflection. Seek feedback from your colleagues, mentors, and clients. They can provide valuable insights into your performance and offer suggestions for improvement. Constructive criticism is a

powerful tool for growth.

4. **Set Bigger Goals**: As you grow in your sales career, your goals should grow with you. If you've reached a milestone, don't settle. Aim higher. Whether it's closing bigger deals, taking on leadership roles, or improving your personal brand, challenge yourself to continue reaching for new heights.

Celebrate, Reflect, Recharge, and Keep Growing

Sales isn't just about hitting targets and closing deals—it's about the journey, the growth, and the continuous process of learning and evolving. Success is a result of hard work, perseverance, and a mindset of continuous improvement. By celebrating your wins, reflecting on your experiences, taking time to recharge, and focusing on growth, you ensure that you're not only successful today but will continue to be successful tomorrow.

So, take a moment to celebrate your victories. Reflect on your journey, learn from your experiences, and recharge for the next challenge. Keep growing and evolving, because the best is always yet to come. Success in sales is not a destination—it's a continuous journey of self-improvement, and you're just getting started.

The Finale

Keep Selling, Girl!

And there you have it—the ultimate guide to owning your sales game, step by step. But let's be real: This isn't the end. It's just the beginning. Being a top-notch salesperson isn't something that happens overnight, and it's not a destination—it's a continuous journey. Every conversation you have, every deal you close, and every challenge you face is an opportunity for growth, learning, and leveling up. You've got the tools, the mindset, and the skills to thrive, and now it's time to put them into action.

Throughout this book, we've covered everything from understanding your product inside and out to mastering the art of building relationships, handling objections, and closing deals with confidence. You've learned how to communicate effectively, how to stay motivated, and how to bounce back from setbacks. You've even explored the importance of celebrating your successes and reflecting on your journey. So, now that you've got the knowledge and the strategies, what's next?

It's time to *own* it.

Don't wait for the perfect moment, the ideal conditions, or for someone else to tell you you're ready. You're already ready. The sales world is yours to conquer, and there's no limit to what you can achieve. Whether you're starting your own business, climbing the corporate ladder, or building a side hustle, the skills you've learned in this book will serve as your foundation. But remember—this is a living, breathing process. You'll always learn, adapt, and improve as you go.

So, go out there and show them what you've got! Be bold. Be confident. And, most importantly, be yourself. There will be highs and lows along the way, but if you stay focused, stay consistent, and keep pushing forward, you'll keep winning. Don't let any "no" hold you back. Turn every rejection into a lesson, and every success into a springboard for the next one.

At the end of the day, you're more than just a salesperson. You're a relationship builder, a problem-solver, a trusted advisor, and a go-getter. You've got everything it takes to sell with integrity, build trust, and create lasting connections that turn customers into loyal fans. So keep selling, girl, because there's no one who can do it like you!

Now, go out there and own your sales journey. You've got this. Keep selling, keep growing, and keep crushing it—because girl, *you can sell!*

Empowering Books on Selling

1. **"The Confidence Code: The Science and Art of Self-Assurance—What Women Should Know"** by Katty Kay and Claire Shipman

    This book dives into the science behind confidence, offering women practical advice on how to harness their self-assurance in every aspect of their life, including sales.

2. **"Girlboss"** by Sophia Amoruso

    A great read for women looking to break through the barriers of business and sales. Sophia shares her personal journey and insights on entrepreneurship and succeeding on your own terms.

3. **"Sell Like a Woman: The Art of Selling When There Are No Rules"** by Shari Levitin

    In this book, Shari Levitin discusses how women can leverage their unique strengths to thrive in sales, offering strategies to build relationships and trust with customers.

4. **"The Challenger Sale: Taking Control of the Customer Conversation"** by Matthew Dixon and Brent Adamson

    Although not specifically for women, this book focuses on the "Challenger" method, which is highly effective in sales. Women can benefit from the insight into how to take control of sales conversations and create value for their customers.

5. "You Are a Badass at Making Money: Master the Mindset of Wealth" by Jen Sincero

This book isn't just about selling—it's about embracing a mindset that drives success. Jen provides actionable advice on overcoming fear and self-doubt in sales while empowering women to make money on their own terms.

6. "The Ultimate Sales Machine: Turbocharge Your Business with Relentless Focus on 12 Key Strategies" by Chet Holmes

A comprehensive guide for anyone in sales, offering a strategic approach that women can adapt to achieve success in sales by focusing on proven methods and continual improvement.

7. "She Means Business: Turn Your Ideas into Reality and Become a Wildly Successful Entrepreneur" by Carrie Green

A fantastic guide for female entrepreneurs, this book helps women in sales (and business) master their mindset, leverage their potential, and create lasting success.

8. "Pitch Like a Girl: How to Use Your Femininity to Succeed in Business" by Ronna Lichtenberg

This book empowers women to embrace their unique qualities and use them as tools to connect with clients and sell with authenticity and grace.

9. "Sell with a Story: How to Capture Attention, Build Trust, and Close the Sale" by Paul Smith

Women can benefit from learning the art of

storytelling in sales. This book provides a framework for creating compelling stories that can make a lasting impact on customers and prospects.

10. "Women Who Lead: Empowering Women in Leadership and Sales" by Shirley Taylor

This book explores the dynamics of women in leadership roles and sales, offering strategies to lead with confidence, overcome challenges, and succeed in male-dominated industries.

30 Empowering Affirmations For Women in Sales

1. I am confident in my ability to sell and create lasting relationships.
2. Every "no" brings me closer to a "yes."
3. I trust in my skills and knowledge to guide me toward success.
4. I am a valuable asset to my clients and can help them solve their problems.
5. I believe in my products and services, and that belief shines through in every conversation.
6. My worth as a saleswoman is not defined by a single outcome, but by my ongoing efforts.
7. I am a natural communicator who listens deeply and speaks with purpose.

8. I attract the right clients who value what I offer.

9. I confidently ask for the sale, knowing I am providing value.

10. I turn challenges into opportunities for growth and improvement.

11. I am resilient, and I bounce back from setbacks stronger than before.

12. I trust that my hard work will lead to success and fulfillment.

13. I am capable of achieving my sales goals and exceeding expectations.

14. Every conversation is a chance to build trust and strengthen relationships.

15. I am proud of my ability to close deals with confidence and integrity.

16. I am worthy of success, wealth, and recognition in my career.

17. I celebrate every small victory and use it as motivation for future success.

18. I know my product inside and out, and I share that knowledge with confidence.

19. I am constantly learning, growing, and evolving in my sales career.

20. I am a powerful negotiator who creates win-win situations for all.

21. I remain calm and confident in the face of objections, turning them into opportunities.

22. I attract clients who value my expertise and are eager to work with me.

23. I trust my intuition to guide me in making the right sales decisions.

24. I am a successful saleswoman, and my success is a reflection of my hard work and dedication.

25. I communicate with clarity, conviction, and compassion in every interaction.

26. I embrace every challenge as an opportunity to refine my skills.

27. I am in control of my sales process, and I make it work for me.

28. I build genuine connections with my clients that last long after the sale.

29. I am confident in my unique strengths and abilities as a woman in sales.

30. I celebrate my progress and trust that each step brings me closer to my goals.

These affirmations will help reinforce a positive mindset, boost confidence, and help you in sales to stay motivated as you pursue your goals.

About the Author

Dr. Monique Rodgers is an international bestselling author, CEO, visionary, master business coach, certified vegan health coach, motivational speaker, entrepreneur, educator, Mary Kay independent advanced color & skin care consultant and literary genius. Dr. Rodgers excels today as a notable writing coach, founder, and serial entrepreneur. Throughout the course of her career, she has written such prolific works such as Hello! My name is Millennial. Picking up the Pieces, The Mystical Land of Twinville, Falling in Love with Jesus, Accelerate, Overcoming Writer's Block, Just Breathe, Called to Intercede Volumes 1-14 and I am Black History and many more. She has also been included as a co-author in collaborations such as Jumpstart Your Mind, Speak Up We Deserve to be Heard, Finding Joy in the Journey Volume 2, and Let the Kingdompreneurs Speak. Due to her outstanding breadth of experience, Dr. Rodgers has been featured on Rachel Speaks radio program, The Love Walk Podcast, The Glory Network, God's Glory Radio Show, The Miracle Zone, The Healing Zone, The Joyce Kiwani Adams Show, Coach Monique Ph.D. radio show, and many more. She has graced numerous platforms worldwide. She served as a TV host for WATCTV. She has been featured in Heart and

Soul magazine, My Story the Magazine, and Kish Magazine's Top 20 Authors of 2021. She has also been featured in Marquis Who's Who in America 2021-2022. She also assisted in various volunteer work including an executive team member for Lady Deliverers Arise, Aniyah Space, and a board member for the I Am My Sister organization. She is also a certified master business coach, certified vegan health coach, and a health advocate. She has served in various leadership positions in business and in ministry. She is currently an Awakening Prayer hub leader for the city of Raleigh under the tutelage of Apostle Jennifer LeClaire. She is an ambassador for Kingdom Sniper Institute under the mentorship of Evangelist Latrice Ryan. As an expert in her field, Dr. Rodgers earned an undergraduate degree through Oral Roberts University as well as a Master of Science degree and a doctorate in global leadership through Colorado Technical University. She has also studied at The Black Business School online. Looking towards her future, Dr. Rodgers intends to expand upon her expertise and continue serving through ministry for God. She aspires to help over one hundred authors to complete and publish their books, help intercessors to draw closer to God and help train marketplace prophets and leaders for success.

To stay connected with Dr. Monique Rodgers

Contact information:
www.getwriteoncoaching.com
www.meetdrmonique.com
Facebook: www.facebook.com/moniquerodgers2
Instagram: @drroyalty7
Twitter: @DrMonique7
LinkedIn: Dr. Monique Rodgers
YouTube: Dr. Monique Rodgers
Clubhouse: @DrMonique7
Email: calledtointerecede@gmail.com

www.ingramcontent.com/pod-product-compliance
Lightning Source LLC
Chambersburg PA
CBHW071550220526
45469CB00003B/970